Discrete Password Logbook: "Kitty Cats" Edition

ISBN: 978-1-64594-040-1

Published by Suzeteo Enterprises, 2019. All Rights Reserved.

Quantities of 500 or more can be purchased in bulk by emailing bulk@suzeteo.com

SAMPLE

	C
Name: Chester Bank	**Updated Passwords:**
URL: www.samplebank.com	
Username: holycats9	
Password: 45T#9111	
Notes: Mom's bank. Security pin: 9871 Recovery answer: kittens	
Name: Credit Card	**Updated Passwords:**
URL: www.samplebank.com	~~Apparentlytheywill12~~
Username: holycats99	~~Wowtheyaregood98%~~
Password: ~~Youhackerswillneverguessthis!~~	5frxdds0%%%&9!
Notes: Hackers keep breaking into the credit card's website!	

A

Name:	Updated Passwords:
URL:	
Username:	
Password:	
Notes:	

Name:	Updated Passwords:
URL:	
Username:	
Password:	
Notes:	

A

Name:	Updated Passwords:
URL:	
Username:	
Password:	
Notes:	

Name:	Updated Passwords:
URL:	
Username:	
Password:	
Notes:	

Name:	Updated Passwords:
URL:	
Username:	
Password:	
Notes:	

A

Name:	Updated Passwords:
URL:	
Username:	
Password:	
Notes:	

Name:	Updated Passwords:
URL:	
Username:	
Password:	
Notes:	

Name:	Updated Passwords:
URL:	
Username:	
Password:	
Notes:	

A

Name:	Updated Passwords:
URL:	
Username:	
Password:	
Notes:	

Name:	Updated Passwords:
URL:	
Username:	
Password:	
Notes:	

Name:	Updated Passwords:
URL:	
Username:	
Password:	
Notes:	

B

Name:	Updated Passwords:
URL:	
Username:	
Password:	
Notes:	

Name:	Updated Passwords:
URL:	
Username:	
Password:	
Notes:	

B

Name:	Updated Passwords:
URL:	
Username:	
Password:	
Notes:	

Name:	Updated Passwords:
URL:	
Username:	
Password:	
Notes:	

Name:	Updated Passwords:
URL:	
Username:	
Password:	
Notes:	

	B
Name:	Updated Passwords:
URL:	
Username:	
Password:	
Notes:	
Name:	Updated Passwords:
URL:	
Username:	
Password:	
Notes:	
Name:	Updated Passwords:
URL:	
Username:	
Password:	
Notes:	

B

Name:	Updated Passwords:
URL:	
Username:	
Password:	
Notes:	

Name:	Updated Passwords:
URL:	
Username:	
Password:	
Notes:	

Name:	Updated Passwords:
URL:	
Username:	
Password:	
Notes:	

C

Name:	Updated Passwords:
URL:	
Username:	
Password:	
Notes:	

Name:	Updated Passwords:
URL:	
Username:	
Password:	
Notes:	

C

Name:	Updated Passwords:
URL:	
Username:	
Password:	
Notes:	

Name:	Updated Passwords:
URL:	
Username:	
Password:	
Notes:	

Name:	Updated Passwords:
URL:	
Username:	
Password:	
Notes:	

C

Name:	Updated Passwords:
URL:	
Username:	
Password:	
Notes:	

Name:	Updated Passwords:
URL:	
Username:	
Password:	
Notes:	

Name:	Updated Passwords:
URL:	
Username:	
Password:	
Notes:	

C

Name:	Updated Passwords:
URL:	
Username:	
Password:	
Notes:	

Name:	Updated Passwords:
URL:	
Username:	
Password:	
Notes:	

Name:	Updated Passwords:
URL:	
Username:	
Password:	
Notes:	

D

Name:	Updated Passwords:
URL:	
Username:	
Password:	
Notes:	

Name:	Updated Passwords:
URL:	
Username:	
Password:	
Notes:	

D

Name:	Updated Passwords:
URL:	
Username:	
Password:	
Notes:	

Name:	Updated Passwords:
URL:	
Username:	
Password:	
Notes:	

Name:	Updated Passwords:
URL:	
Username:	
Password:	
Notes:	

	D
Name:	**Updated Passwords:**
URL:	
Username:	
Password:	
Notes:	
Name:	**Updated Passwords:**
URL:	
Username:	
Password:	
Notes:	
Name:	**Updated Passwords:**
URL:	
Username:	
Password:	
Notes:	

D

Name:	Updated Passwords:
URL:	
Username:	
Password:	
Notes:	

Name:	Updated Passwords:
URL:	
Username:	
Password:	
Notes:	

Name:	Updated Passwords:
URL:	
Username:	
Password:	
Notes:	

E

Name:	Updated Passwords:
URL:	
Username:	
Password:	
Notes:	

Name:	Updated Passwords:
URL:	
Username:	
Password:	
Notes:	

E

Name:	Updated Passwords:
URL:	
Username:	
Password:	
Notes:	

Name:	Updated Passwords:
URL:	
Username:	
Password:	
Notes:	

Name:	Updated Passwords:
URL:	
Username:	
Password:	
Notes:	

	E
Name:	Updated Passwords:
URL:	
Username:	
Password:	
Notes:	
Name:	Updated Passwords:
URL:	
Username:	
Password:	
Notes:	
Name:	Updated Passwords:
URL:	
Username:	
Password:	
Notes:	

E

Name:	Updated Passwords:
URL:	
Username:	
Password:	
Notes:	

Name:	Updated Passwords:
URL:	
Username:	
Password:	
Notes:	

Name:	Updated Passwords:
URL:	
Username:	
Password:	
Notes:	

F

Name:	Updated Passwords:
URL:	
Username:	
Password:	
Notes:	

Name:	Updated Passwords:
URL:	
Username:	
Password:	
Notes:	

F

Name:	Updated Passwords:
URL:	
Username:	
Password:	
Notes:	

Name:	Updated Passwords:
URL:	
Username:	
Password:	
Notes:	

Name:	Updated Passwords:
URL:	
Username:	
Password:	
Notes:	

	F
Name:	Updated Passwords:
URL:	
Username:	
Password:	
Notes:	

Name:	Updated Passwords:
URL:	
Username:	
Password:	
Notes:	

Name:	Updated Passwords:
URL:	
Username:	
Password:	
Notes:	

F

Name:	Updated Passwords:
URL:	
Username:	
Password:	
Notes:	

Name:	Updated Passwords:
URL:	
Username:	
Password:	
Notes:	

Name:	Updated Passwords:
URL:	
Username:	
Password:	
Notes:	

G

Name:	Updated Passwords:
URL:	
Username:	
Password:	
Notes:	

Name:	Updated Passwords:
URL:	
Username:	
Password:	
Notes:	

G

Name:	Updated Passwords:
URL:	
Username:	
Password:	
Notes:	

Name:	Updated Passwords:
URL:	
Username:	
Password:	
Notes:	

Name:	Updated Passwords:
URL:	
Username:	
Password:	
Notes:	

G

Name:	Updated Passwords:
URL:	
Username:	
Password:	
Notes:	

Name:	Updated Passwords:
URL:	
Username:	
Password:	
Notes:	

Name:	Updated Passwords:
URL:	
Username:	
Password:	
Notes:	

G

Name:	Updated Passwords:
URL:	
Username:	
Password:	
Notes:	

Name:	Updated Passwords:
URL:	
Username:	
Password:	
Notes:	

Name:	Updated Passwords:
URL:	
Username:	
Password:	
Notes:	

H

Name:	Updated Passwords:
URL:	
Username:	
Password:	
Notes:	

Name:	Updated Passwords:
URL:	
Username:	
Password:	
Notes:	

H

Name:	Updated Passwords:
URL:	
Username:	
Password:	
Notes:	

Name:	Updated Passwords:
URL:	
Username:	
Password:	
Notes:	

Name:	Updated Passwords:
URL:	
Username:	
Password:	
Notes:	

	H
Name:	Updated Passwords:
URL:	
Username:	
Password:	
Notes:	
Name:	Updated Passwords:
URL:	
Username:	
Password:	
Notes:	
Name:	Updated Passwords:
URL:	
Username:	
Password:	
Notes:	

H

Name:	Updated Passwords:
URL:	
Username:	
Password:	
Notes:	

Name:	Updated Passwords:
URL:	
Username:	
Password:	
Notes:	

Name:	Updated Passwords:
URL:	
Username:	
Password:	
Notes:	

1

Name:	Updated Passwords:
URL:	
Username:	
Password:	
Notes:	

Name:	Updated Passwords:
URL:	
Username:	
Password:	
Notes:	

Name:	**Updated Passwords:**
URL:	
Username:	
Password:	
Notes:	

Name:	**Updated Passwords:**
URL:	
Username:	
Password:	
Notes:	

Name:	**Updated Passwords:**
URL:	
Username:	
Password:	
Notes:	

Name:	Updated Passwords:
URL:	
Username:	
Password:	
Notes:	

Name:	Updated Passwords:
URL:	
Username:	
Password:	
Notes:	

Name:	Updated Passwords:
URL:	
Username:	
Password:	
Notes:	

(	
Name:	**Updated Passwords:**
URL:	
Username:	
Password:	
Notes:	

Name:	**Updated Passwords:**
URL:	
Username:	
Password:	
Notes:	

Name:	**Updated Passwords:**
URL:	
Username:	
Password:	
Notes:	

Name:	Updated Passwords:
URL:	
Username:	
Password:	
Notes:	

Name:	Updated Passwords:
URL:	
Username:	
Password:	
Notes:	

Name:	**Updated Passwords:**
URL:	
Username:	
Password:	
Notes:	

Name:	**Updated Passwords:**
URL:	
Username:	
Password:	
Notes:	

Name:	**Updated Passwords:**
URL:	
Username:	
Password:	
Notes:	

	J
Name:	Updated Passwords:
URL:	
Username:	
Password:	
Notes:	

Name:	Updated Passwords:
URL:	
Username:	
Password:	
Notes:	

Name:	Updated Passwords:
URL:	
Username:	
Password:	
Notes:	

J

Name:	Updated Passwords:
URL:	
Username:	
Password:	
Notes:	

Name:	Updated Passwords:
URL:	
Username:	
Password:	
Notes:	

Name:	Updated Passwords:
URL:	
Username:	
Password:	
Notes:	

K

Name:	Updated Passwords:
URL:	
Username:	
Password:	
Notes:	

Name:	Updated Passwords:
URL:	
Username:	
Password:	
Notes:	

K

Name:	Updated Passwords:
URL:	
Username:	
Password:	
Notes:	

Name:	Updated Passwords:
URL:	
Username:	
Password:	
Notes:	

Name:	Updated Passwords:
URL:	
Username:	
Password:	
Notes:	

	K
Name:	Updated Passwords:
URL:	
Username:	
Password:	
Notes:	

Name:	Updated Passwords:
URL:	
Username:	
Password:	
Notes:	

Name:	Updated Passwords:
URL:	
Username:	
Password:	
Notes:	

K

Name:	Updated Passwords:
URL:	
Username:	
Password:	
Notes:	

Name:	Updated Passwords:
URL:	
Username:	
Password:	
Notes:	

Name:	Updated Passwords:
URL:	
Username:	
Password:	
Notes:	

L

Name:	Updated Passwords:
URL:	
Username:	
Password:	
Notes:	

Name:	Updated Passwords:
URL:	
Username:	
Password:	
Notes:	

L

Name:	Updated Passwords:
URL:	
Username:	
Password:	
Notes:	

Name:	Updated Passwords:
URL:	
Username:	
Password:	
Notes:	

Name:	Updated Passwords:
URL:	
Username:	
Password:	
Notes:	

	L
Name:	Updated Passwords:
URL:	
Username:	
Password:	
Notes:	

Name:	Updated Passwords:
URL:	
Username:	
Password:	
Notes:	

Name:	Updated Passwords:
URL:	
Username:	
Password:	
Notes:	

L

Name:	Updated Passwords:
URL:	
Username:	
Password:	
Notes:	

Name:	Updated Passwords:
URL:	
Username:	
Password:	
Notes:	

Name:	Updated Passwords:
URL:	
Username:	
Password:	
Notes:	

M

Name:	Updated Passwords:
URL:	
Username:	
Password:	
Notes:	

Name:	Updated Passwords:
URL:	
Username:	
Password:	
Notes:	

M

Name:	Updated Passwords:
URL:	
Username:	
Password:	
Notes:	

Name:	Updated Passwords:
URL:	
Username:	
Password:	
Notes:	

Name:	Updated Passwords:
URL:	
Username:	
Password:	
Notes:	

	M
Name:	Updated Passwords:
URL:	
Username:	
Password:	
Notes:	

Name:	Updated Passwords:
URL:	
Username:	
Password:	
Notes:	

Name:	Updated Passwords:
URL:	
Username:	
Password:	
Notes:	

M

Name:	Updated Passwords:
URL:	
Username:	
Password:	
Notes:	

Name:	Updated Passwords:
URL:	
Username:	
Password:	
Notes:	

Name:	Updated Passwords:
URL:	
Username:	
Password:	
Notes:	

N

Name:	Updated Passwords:
URL:	
Username:	
Password:	
Notes:	

Name:	Updated Passwords:
URL:	
Username:	
Password:	
Notes:	

N

Name:	Updated Passwords:
URL:	
Username:	
Password:	
Notes:	

Name:	Updated Passwords:
URL:	
Username:	
Password:	
Notes:	

Name:	Updated Passwords:
URL:	
Username:	
Password:	
Notes:	

N

Name:	Updated Passwords:
URL:	
Username:	
Password:	
Notes:	

Name:	Updated Passwords:
URL:	
Username:	
Password:	
Notes:	

Name:	Updated Passwords:
URL:	
Username:	
Password:	
Notes:	

N

Name:	Updated Passwords:
URL:	
Username:	
Password:	
Notes:	

Name:	Updated Passwords:
URL:	
Username:	
Password:	
Notes:	

Name:	Updated Passwords:
URL:	
Username:	
Password:	
Notes:	

Name:	Updated Passwords:
URL:	
Username:	
Password:	
Notes:	

Name:	Updated Passwords:
URL:	
Username:	
Password:	
Notes:	

	Updated Passwords:
Name:	
URL:	
Username:	
Password:	
Notes:	

	Updated Passwords:
Name:	
URL:	
Username:	
Password:	
Notes:	

	Updated Passwords:
Name:	
URL:	
Username:	
Password:	
Notes:	

Name:	Updated Passwords:
URL:	
Username:	
Password:	
Notes:	

Name:	Updated Passwords:
URL:	
Username:	
Password:	
Notes:	

Name:	Updated Passwords:
URL:	
Username:	
Password:	
Notes:	

Name:	Updated Passwords:
URL:	
Username:	
Password:	
Notes:	

Name:	Updated Passwords:
URL:	
Username:	
Password:	
Notes:	

Name:	Updated Passwords:
URL:	
Username:	
Password:	
Notes:	

P

Name:	Updated Passwords:
URL:	
Username:	
Password:	
Notes:	

Name:	Updated Passwords:
URL:	
Username:	
Password:	
Notes:	

P

Name:	Updated Passwords:
URL:	
Username:	
Password:	
Notes:	

Name:	Updated Passwords:
URL:	
Username:	
Password:	
Notes:	

Name:	Updated Passwords:
URL:	
Username:	
Password:	
Notes:	

	P
Name:	**Updated Passwords:**
URL:	
Username:	
Password:	
Notes:	
Name:	**Updated Passwords:**
URL:	
Username:	
Password:	
Notes:	
Name:	**Updated Passwords:**
URL:	
Username:	
Password:	
Notes:	

P

Name:	Updated Passwords:
URL:	
Username:	
Password:	
Notes:	

Name:	Updated Passwords:
URL:	
Username:	
Password:	
Notes:	

Name:	Updated Passwords:
URL:	
Username:	
Password:	
Notes:	

Q

Name:	Updated Passwords:
URL:	
Username:	
Password:	
Notes:	

Name:	Updated Passwords:
URL:	
Username:	
Password:	
Notes:	

Q

Name:	Updated Passwords:
URL:	
Username:	
Password:	
Notes:	

Name:	Updated Passwords:
URL:	
Username:	
Password:	
Notes:	

Name:	Updated Passwords:
URL:	
Username:	
Password:	
Notes:	

Name:	Updated Passwords:
URL:	
Username:	
Password:	
Notes:	

Name:	Updated Passwords:
URL:	
Username:	
Password:	
Notes:	

Name:	Updated Passwords:
URL:	
Username:	
Password:	
Notes:	

Q

Name:	Updated Passwords:
URL:	
Username:	
Password:	
Notes:	

Name:	Updated Passwords:
URL:	
Username:	
Password:	
Notes:	

Name:	Updated Passwords:
URL:	
Username:	
Password:	
Notes:	

R

Name:	Updated Passwords:
URL:	
Username:	
Password:	
Notes:	

Name:	Updated Passwords:
URL:	
Username:	
Password:	
Notes:	

R

Name:	Updated Passwords:
URL:	
Username:	
Password:	
Notes:	

Name:	Updated Passwords:
URL:	
Username:	
Password:	
Notes:	

Name:	Updated Passwords:
URL:	
Username:	
Password:	
Notes:	

R

Name:	Updated Passwords:
URL:	
Username:	
Password:	
Notes:	

Name:	Updated Passwords:
URL:	
Username:	
Password:	
Notes:	

Name:	Updated Passwords:
URL:	
Username:	
Password:	
Notes:	

R

Name:	Updated Passwords:
URL:	
Username:	
Password:	
Notes:	

Name:	Updated Passwords:
URL:	
Username:	
Password:	
Notes:	

Name:	Updated Passwords:
URL:	
Username:	
Password:	
Notes:	

S

Name:	Updated Passwords:
URL:	
Username:	
Password:	
Notes:	

Name:	Updated Passwords:
URL:	
Username:	
Password:	
Notes:	

S

Name:	Updated Passwords:
URL:	
Username:	
Password:	
Notes:	

Name:	Updated Passwords:
URL:	
Username:	
Password:	
Notes:	

Name:	Updated Passwords:
URL:	
Username:	
Password:	
Notes:	

	S
Name:	Updated Passwords:
URL:	
Username:	
Password:	
Notes:	

Name:	Updated Passwords:
URL:	
Username:	
Password:	
Notes:	

Name:	Updated Passwords:
URL:	
Username:	
Password:	
Notes:	

S

Name:	Updated Passwords:
URL:	
Username:	
Password:	
Notes:	

Name:	Updated Passwords:
URL:	
Username:	
Password:	
Notes:	

Name:	Updated Passwords:
URL:	
Username:	
Password:	
Notes:	

T

Name:	Updated Passwords:
URL:	
Username:	
Password:	
Notes:	

Name:	Updated Passwords:
URL:	
Username:	
Password:	
Notes:	

T

Name:	Updated Passwords:
URL:	
Username:	
Password:	
Notes:	

Name:	Updated Passwords:
URL:	
Username:	
Password:	
Notes:	

Name:	Updated Passwords:
URL:	
Username:	
Password:	
Notes:	

	T
Name:	Updated Passwords:
URL:	
Username:	
Password:	
Notes:	

Name:	Updated Passwords:
URL:	
Username:	
Password:	
Notes:	

Name:	Updated Passwords:
URL:	
Username:	
Password:	
Notes:	

T

Name:	Updated Passwords:
URL:	
Username:	
Password:	
Notes:	

Name:	Updated Passwords:
URL:	
Username:	
Password:	
Notes:	

Name:	Updated Passwords:
URL:	
Username:	
Password:	
Notes:	

U

Name:	Updated Passwords:
URL:	
Username:	
Password:	
Notes:	

Name:	Updated Passwords:
URL:	
Username:	
Password:	
Notes:	

U

Name:	Updated Passwords:
URL:	
Username:	
Password:	
Notes:	

Name:	Updated Passwords:
URL:	
Username:	
Password:	
Notes:	

Name:	Updated Passwords:
URL:	
Username:	
Password:	
Notes:	

	U
Name:	**Updated Passwords:**
URL:	
Username:	
Password:	
Notes:	

Name:	**Updated Passwords:**
URL:	
Username:	
Password:	
Notes:	

Name:	**Updated Passwords:**
URL:	
Username:	
Password:	
Notes:	

U

Name:	Updated Passwords:
URL:	
Username:	
Password:	
Notes:	

Name:	Updated Passwords:
URL:	
Username:	
Password:	
Notes:	

Name:	Updated Passwords:
URL:	
Username:	
Password:	
Notes:	

V

Name:	Updated Passwords:
URL:	
Username:	
Password:	
Notes:	

Name:	Updated Passwords:
URL:	
Username:	
Password:	
Notes:	

V

Name:	Updated Passwords:
URL:	
Username:	
Password:	
Notes:	

Name:	Updated Passwords:
URL:	
Username:	
Password:	
Notes:	

Name:	Updated Passwords:
URL:	
Username:	
Password:	
Notes:	

V

Name:	Updated Passwords:
URL:	
Username:	
Password:	
Notes:	

Name:	Updated Passwords:
URL:	
Username:	
Password:	
Notes:	

Name:	Updated Passwords:
URL:	
Username:	
Password:	
Notes:	

V

Name:	Updated Passwords:
URL:	
Username:	
Password:	
Notes:	

Name:	Updated Passwords:
URL:	
Username:	
Password:	
Notes:	

Name:	Updated Passwords:
URL:	
Username:	
Password:	
Notes:	

W

Name:	Updated Passwords:
URL:	
Username:	
Password:	
Notes:	

Name:	Updated Passwords:
URL:	
Username:	
Password:	
Notes:	

W

Name:	Updated Passwords:
URL:	
Username:	
Password:	
Notes:	

Name:	Updated Passwords:
URL:	
Username:	
Password:	
Notes:	

Name:	Updated Passwords:
URL:	
Username:	
Password:	
Notes:	

	W
Name:	**Updated Passwords:**
URL:	
Username:	
Password:	
Notes:	

Name:	**Updated Passwords:**
URL:	
Username:	
Password:	
Notes:	

Name:	**Updated Passwords:**
URL:	
Username:	
Password:	
Notes:	

W

Name:	Updated Passwords:
URL:	
Username:	
Password:	
Notes:	

Name:	Updated Passwords:
URL:	
Username:	
Password:	
Notes:	

Name:	Updated Passwords:
URL:	
Username:	
Password:	
Notes:	

Name:	Updated Passwords:
URL:	
Username:	
Password:	
Notes:	

Name:	Updated Passwords:
URL:	
Username:	
Password:	
Notes:	

✕	
Name:	Updated Passwords:
URL:	
Username:	
Password:	
Notes:	

Name:	Updated Passwords:
URL:	
Username:	
Password:	
Notes:	

Name:	Updated Passwords:
URL:	
Username:	
Password:	
Notes:	

	X
Name:	**Updated Passwords:**
URL:	
Username:	
Password:	
Notes:	

Name:	**Updated Passwords:**
URL:	
Username:	
Password:	
Notes:	

Name:	**Updated Passwords:**
URL:	
Username:	
Password:	
Notes:	

✕	
Name:	**Updated Passwords:**
URL:	
Username:	
Password:	
Notes:	

Name:	**Updated Passwords:**
URL:	
Username:	
Password:	
Notes:	

Name:	**Updated Passwords:**
URL:	
Username:	
Password:	
Notes:	

Y

Name:	Updated Passwords:
URL:	
Username:	
Password:	
Notes:	

Name:	Updated Passwords:
URL:	
Username:	
Password:	
Notes:	

Y

Name:	Updated Passwords:
URL:	
Username:	
Password:	
Notes:	

Name:	Updated Passwords:
URL:	
Username:	
Password:	
Notes:	

Name:	Updated Passwords:
URL:	
Username:	
Password:	
Notes:	

	Y
Name:	Updated Passwords:
URL:	
Username:	
Password:	
Notes:	

Name:	Updated Passwords:
URL:	
Username:	
Password:	
Notes:	

Name:	Updated Passwords:
URL:	
Username:	
Password:	
Notes:	

Y

Name:	Updated Passwords:
URL:	
Username:	
Password:	
Notes:	

Name:	Updated Passwords:
URL:	
Username:	
Password:	
Notes:	

Name:	Updated Passwords:
URL:	
Username:	
Password:	
Notes:	

Z

Name:	Updated Passwords:
URL:	
Username:	
Password:	
Notes:	

Name:	Updated Passwords:
URL:	
Username:	
Password:	
Notes:	

Z

Name:	Updated Passwords:
URL:	
Username:	
Password:	
Notes:	

Name:	Updated Passwords:
URL:	
Username:	
Password:	
Notes:	

Name:	Updated Passwords:
URL:	
Username:	
Password:	
Notes:	

Z

Name:	Updated Passwords:
URL:	
Username:	
Password:	
Notes:	

Name:	Updated Passwords:
URL:	
Username:	
Password:	
Notes:	

Name:	Updated Passwords:
URL:	
Username:	
Password:	
Notes:	

Z

Name:	Updated Passwords:
URL:	
Username:	
Password:	
Notes:	

Name:	Updated Passwords:
URL:	
Username:	
Password:	
Notes:	

Name:	Updated Passwords:
URL:	
Username:	
Password:	
Notes:	

Name:	Updated Passwords:
URL:	
Username:	
Password:	
Notes:	

Name:	Updated Passwords:
URL:	
Username:	
Password:	
Notes:	

✳	
Name:	**Updated Passwords:**
URL:	
Username:	
Password:	
Notes:	

Name:	**Updated Passwords:**
URL:	
Username:	
Password:	
Notes:	

Name:	**Updated Passwords:**
URL:	
Username:	
Password:	
Notes:	

	✲
Name:	Updated Passwords:
URL:	
Username:	
Password:	
Notes:	

Name:	Updated Passwords:
URL:	
Username:	
Password:	
Notes:	

Name:	Updated Passwords:
URL:	
Username:	
Password:	
Notes:	

✳	
Name:	Updated Passwords:
URL:	
Username:	
Password:	
Notes:	

Name:	Updated Passwords:
URL:	
Username:	
Password:	
Notes:	

Name:	Updated Passwords:
URL:	
Username:	
Password:	
Notes:	

CPSIA information can be obtained
at www.ICGtesting.com
Printed in the USA
LVHW100154260122
709449LV00005B/37